The Animals Winter Sleep

by Lynda Graham-Barber
pictures by Nancy Carol Willis

Birdsong Books
Middletown, Delaware

Where do the northern animals sleep
when it's nose-stinging cold
and the snow drifts deep?

Bedded down in the spruce grove,
where the howling winds don't blow.

White-tailed deer

In a hollow log
near the old
fence row.

Snowshoe hare

North American
porcupine

Wedged between the
rocks, sleeping all alone,

Snug together under a
crumbling wall of stone.

Striped skunk

In a mud-and-stick lodge,
shaped like a dome,

American beaver

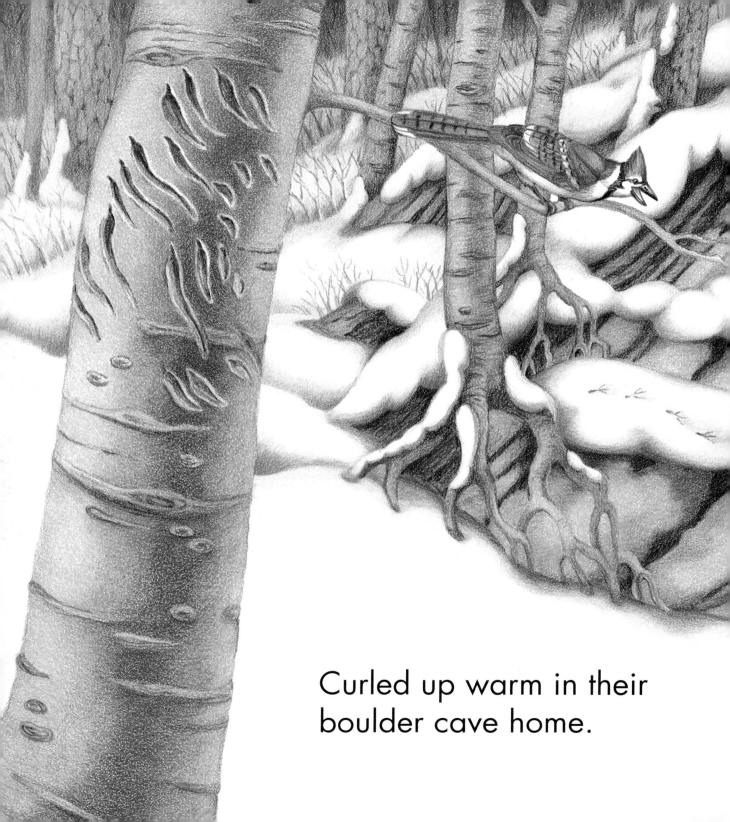

Curled up warm in their
boulder cave home.

Black bear

Northern raccoon

CANDY

Inside a dead maple tree,
with family all around,

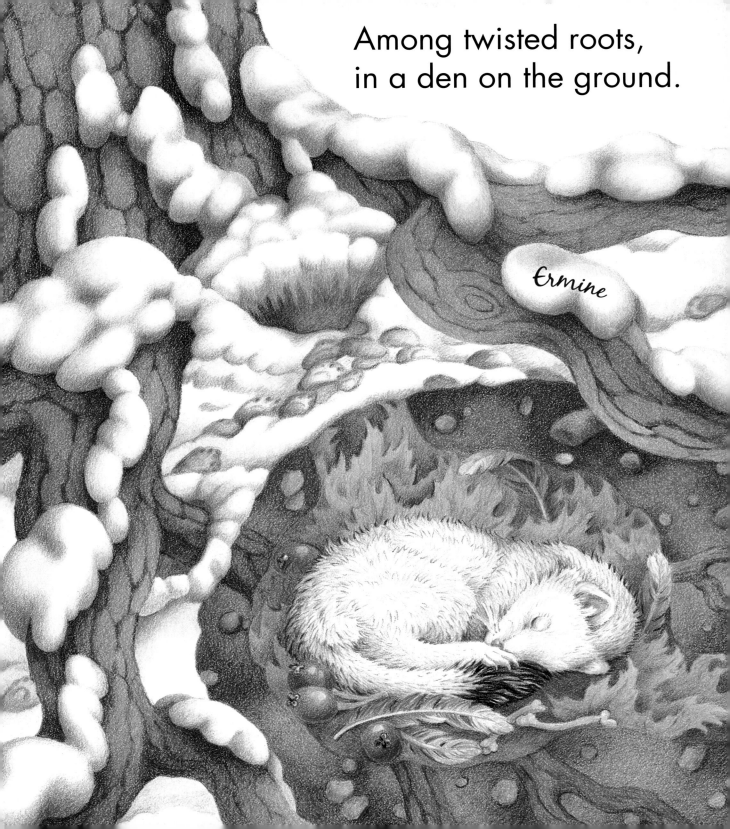

Among twisted roots,
in a den on the ground.

Ermine

Deep in a hillside burrow,
overlooking a farm,

Red fox

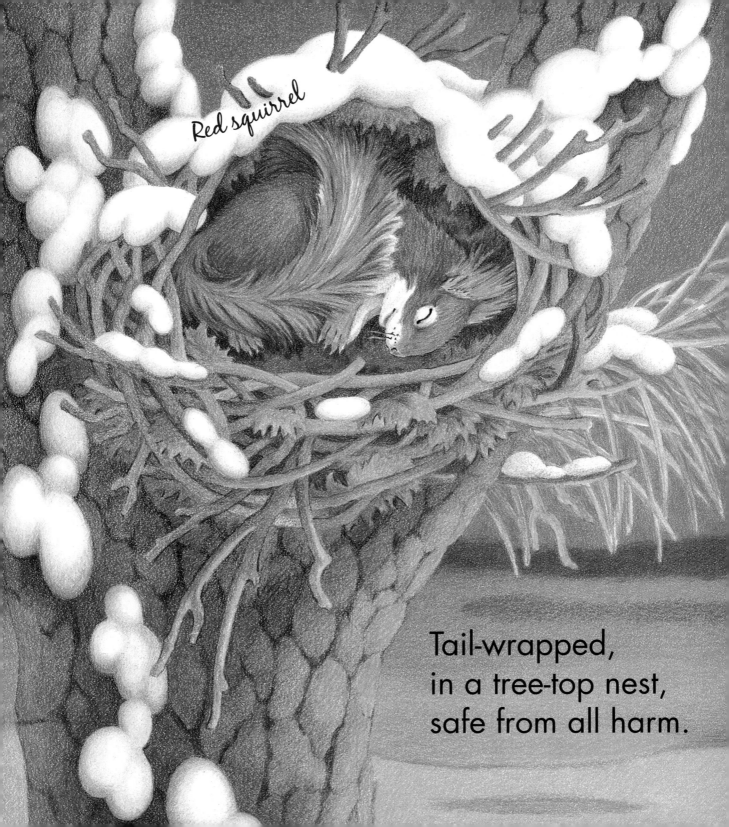

Red squirrel

Tail-wrapped,
in a tree-top nest,
safe from all harm.

Tunneled into the stream bank,
in a leafy, soft nest,

Northern river otter

Pileated woodpecker

In a
chiseled-out
tree hole,
it takes a
night rest.

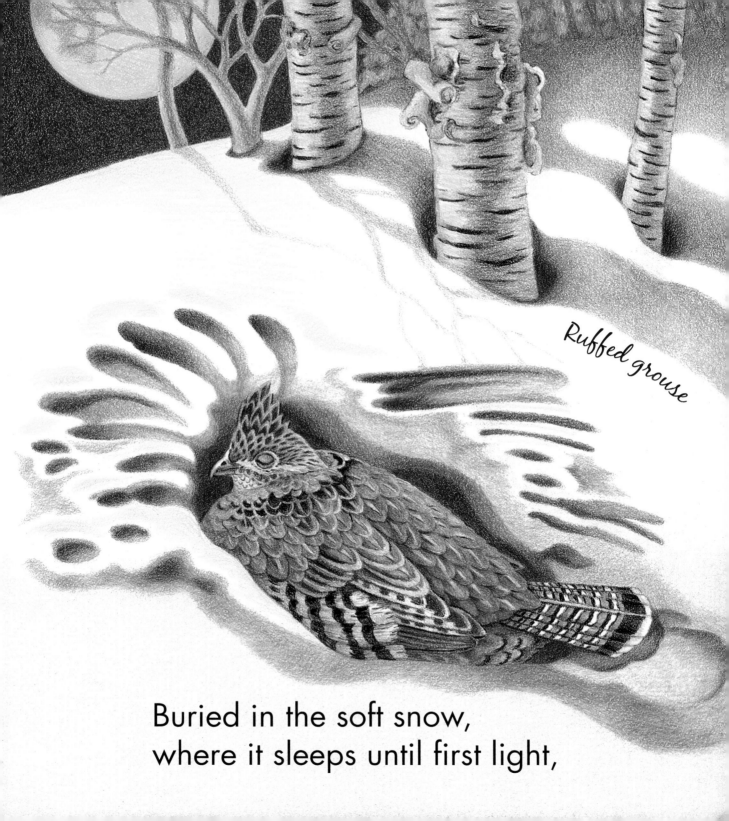

Ruffed grouse

Buried in the soft snow,
where it sleeps until first light,

Sh-h-h, all the animals
are fast asleep tight.
Close your eyes now...
Good winter's snug night.

Imagine sleeping outdoors on a snowy day! How would you keep warm? And what would you eat?

Many northern animals have thick fur coats or downy body feathers, which protect them from the cold. Some line their dens with leaves and soft grasses. Many store food in their dens. Details in the book's pictures hold clues about how 13 different animals survive the icy-cold winter. Look closely at the drawings and have fun answering the questions that follow.

White-tailed deer

Sunrise. As you are waking up, the deer are lying down to sleep. How are the deer protected from the wind? Do you see any food the deer have been eating? Some animals, like the deer, eat plants but no meat. Other animals eat meat, like the coyotes in the distance. Why do you think the mother deer is still awake? She will sleep with her family, after the coyotes leave. Then all the deer will be safe.

Snowshoe hare

Morning. The hare has big, furry feet shaped like snowshoes. How do these feet help the hare move in the snow? The hare's coat is brown in summer. In winter, it turns white. How does the color protect the hare from enemies, like the snowy owl on the fence? What is the hare eating?

North American porcupine

Porcupines tear bark from pine, fir, and hemlock trees, to eat the soft inner bark. The messy porcupine sleeps in its bathroom.

What are the popcorn-shaped objects that have fallen out of the den? There are about 30,000 sharp quills on a porcupine's body. Ouch! Where did some of the quills get stuck?

Striped skunk

Mid-morning. The nocturnal skunk hunts at night for mice, seeds, even garbage. What food has the skunk stored in its "kitchen?" As many as 10 skunks may sleep in an underground den. How many skunks share this den? When attacked, the skunk raises its tail and sprays its enemy with an oily, smelly liquid. Pee yew!

American beaver

Beavers use their sharp front teeth to cut down poplar, willow, and birch trees. Then they build their lodge "house" from these trees and eat the bark, too. Beavers store extra branches in the "refrigerator" at the bottom of the cold, muddy stream. Young beavers live with their parents and grandparents. Do you see the lodge's underwater "door?"

Black bear

Noon. In the winter, the black bear never leaves its den. It does not eat or go to the bathroom all winter long! The bear rests, or hibernates, sleeping on and off. In late winter, the mother bear gives birth to cubs. The newborn cubs snuggle into her belly to nurse on warm milk. Who do you think made the claw marks in the bark of the beech tree?

Northern raccoon

Afternoon. Raccoons may sleep for weeks at a time, but they do not hibernate. On windless nights they leave their den to hunt for dried corn, mice, seeds, and nuts. A raccoon's forepaws are like your hands. Their fingers can open a garbage can and even doors. What kind of food have the raccoons been eating? Where do you think they found this food?

Ermine (Short-tailed weasel)

Ermine sleep alone, curled up like a doughnut. They weigh less than two sticks of butter. But ermine are so strong and fast, they can catch young rabbits for food. What has this ermine been eating? An ermine's fur coat turns from white to brown in the spring. When the ermine's coat is brown, it is called a weasel.

Red Fox

Sunset. The red fox dig a burrow into the hillside. They don't mind living close to people. How can a hilltop home help the fox survive? Inside the burrow, newborn pups nurse on their mother's milk. As the pups grow, their father brings food, like mice and even a woodchuck, to the den. Red fox also eat fruit, sweet corn, and berries.

Red squirrel

What materials have the red squirrel used to make its nest? Red squirrels leave their nests even on cold, snowy days. They dig open underground "pantries." There they have stored favorite foods, like acorns and seeds from pine trees. In late summer, the red squirrel grows long, thick hairs on its ears. How are these ear tufts important in winter? Why does the squirrel sleep with its tail wrapped around its body?

Northern river otter

The playful otters slide down snow banks into the water just for fun. Wheee! Webbed feet, sleek bodies, and tails used for steering make otters powerful swimmers. They catch fish underwater and mice along the shore. Otters dig a den in the banks of a river or pond. They line the den with dried leaves. How many "doors" does the otters' den have?

Pileated woodpecker

Nighttime. This shy woodpecker uses its sharp beak to drill small holes in the tree bark. Rap-tap-tap! It is looking for carpenter ants and other insects to eat. This crow-sized bird also chips out a large hole inside of the tree. There it rests, or roosts, for the night. How does the woodpecker hold onto the sides of the tree when sleeping?

Ruffed grouse

Bedtime. Maybe you are choosing a favorite book to read. That's when the ruffed grouse dives into soft snow. There it will spend the night. The snow acts like a blanket over the earth. So the grouse is warm in its snowy "bed." Do you see the grouse's wing prints on the snow? Have you ever made a snow "angel?"

Were you able to find where all of the animals sleep?

1. Northern raccoon
2. Red fox
3. Snowshoe hare
4. Striped skunk
5. Northern river otter
6. White-tailed deer
7. Ruffed grouse
8. Pileated woodpecker
9. Ermine
10. North American porcupine
11. American beaver
12. Red Squirrel
13. Black bear
14. Children like you!

In loving tribute to Mary Jane Graham - LGB
For Paul, my husband and the joy of my life - NCW

Text copyright © 2008 by Lynda Graham-Barber
Illustrations copyright © 2008 by Nancy Carol Willis

www.BirdsongBooks.com

Library of Congress Control Number 2007942390

Summary: Describes how thirteen northern animal species
survive the winter snug in their dens, burrows, nests and lodges.

ISBN13 978-0-9662761-6-9
ISBN10 09662761-6-7

Printed in China